FIVE CENTURIES
OF GOLF
WISDOM

FIVE CENTURIES
OF GOLF
WISDOM

CHRISTOPHER ARMOUR

Five Centuries of Golf Wisdom by Christopher Armour

 Published by Foxglove Press
1-877-205-1932
© 2006 Foxglove Press

ISBN 1-882959-58-2

Design by Armour&Armour, Nashville, Tennessee
Illustrations by Meredith Green

First Edition 2006
1 2 3 4 5 6 7 8 9 10

To cartoonist Tom Little,
who gave a left-handed
youngster his old clubs
and started my life-long
love of the game of golf

INTRODUCTION

For more than five hundred years, we golfers have chased that single brilliant instant when everything comes together: a sky blue as you've ever seen it, the sun warm, just enough breeze to cool your brow, the smell of new-mown grass jewelled with a hint of dew left from the morning. The world swells until it's just you and a tiny ball perched on a tee.

There's a short moment of peace, of possibility. Then, as you draw back your club, every part of your body is working together (for once), and you know it's a well-hit ball even before you strike it. And then it soars, into the blue and onto the green.

That's what we live for. And that's the spirit I've tried to capture here in *Five Centuries of Golf Wisdom.*

Maybe it's the esssential solitude of man versus ball, or the hours spent honing skills on unfor-giving courses, but golfers seem to be a philo-sophical crowd, musing on everything from their equipment to the course to the nature to the meaning of the game itself.

Not that they take themselves too seriously—I think the game is such a challenge that you have to maintain perspective and keep a sense of humor. You'll find plenty of lighthearted humor among the advice and observations, the history and the histrionics, of golf in the past five centuries.

One thing golf is always aware of is its legacy, the thousands of players who devoted their lives to playing and improving the game. Some of these legends are profiled here as well.

Finally, golf is not usually a team sport, but writing a golf book certainly is. I'd like to thank the foursome who helped make *Five Centuries of Golf Wisdom* possible: Jan Bell and David Harden helped with the writing, Barry Edwards created the cover, and Meredith Green designed the text and created the illustrations.

—Christopher Armour

THE GOLFER'S CREED

Golf is a science, the study of a lifetime, in which you may exhaust yourself, but never your subject. It is a contest, a duel, or a melee, calling for courage, skill, strategy and self-control. It is a test of temper, a trial of honor, a revealer of character. It affords a chance to play the man and act the gentleman. It means going into God's out-of-doors, getting close to nature, fresh air, exercise, a sweeping away of mental cobwebs, genuine recreation of tired tissues. It is a cure for care, an antidote to worry. It includes companionship for friends, social intercourse, opportunities for courtesy, kindliness and generosity to an opponent. It promotes not only physical health but moral force.

DAVID FORGAN

CHAMPIONS

JACK NICKLAUS

Jack Nicklaus, the Golden Bear, is one of golf's greatest icons. He was born on January 21, 1940, in Ohio and began playing golf at age ten. By age nineteen he had won his first U.S. Amateur Championship. His excellent lower body strength combined with tremendous powers of concentration and hours and hours practice to create a golfer whose record is unsurpassed. Fulton Allen said that Nicklaus was the only player he knew who could think and play golf at the same time. He was the youngest to ever win the Masters and has won three Grand Slams.

- *U.S. Amateur 1959, 1961*
- *U.S. Open 1962, 1967, 1972, 1980*
- *Masters 1963, 1965, 1966, 1972, 1975, 1986*
- *British Open 1966, 1970, 1978*
- *PGA 1963, 1971, 1973, 1975, 1980*
- *World Golf Hall of Fame 1974*

Golf is not, and never has been, a fair game.

Jack Nicklaus (1940–)

A SHORT HISTORY OF GOLF

The origins of golf are lost in the sands of time (which now can be found in a bunker at St. Andrews in Scotland).

The Romans played *paganica* with a curved stick and a ball stuffed with feathers, introducing the game to Britain along with empire and aquaducts.

The Dutch played *het kolven*, a game similar to golf played both on land and on ice. But the Scots tell us they had been playing golf for hundreds of years by that point. The name may come from "to gowff," Scottish for "to strike hard."

The earliest written history of golf has its roots in the government of Scotland's trying to stop people from playing. The first recorded mention of the sport is in 1452, when James II banned golf because it kept his subjects from practicing their archery. The ban apparently didn't take, leading to a 1471 ban by James III and a 1491 ban by James IV.

He finally came to his senses and took up the sport himself in 1502, as did his daughter, Mary Queen of Scots, who was on the links the day after her husband was murdered in 1567. (She thus became the first golf widow.)

The men of the kingdom rejoiced in 1618, when James VI allowed his countrymen to play golf on Sundays for the first time. This was the last time wives saw their husbands on the weekend.

Fewer than fifty years later, golf had made it to the new world—and of course was immediately banned from the streets of Albany, New York in 1659.

In 1682, the first known international golf match was played at Leith, Scotland. All the participants are not known, but Andrew Dickson carried someone's clubs and became the first known caddie.

The rules of modern golf trace their roots to the Honorable Company of Edinburgh golfers, formed in the town of Leith. The group created the first written rules in 1744. Ten years later, the St. Andrews Society took over maintenance and development of the game shortly thereafter, and, as the Royal and Ancient Golf Club of St. Andrews, remains in control of rules and standards more than two hundred fifty years later.

The first open championship on the old course was played in 1754. Five years later, the first game determined by stroke play was recorded; before that, all play was match.

In 1764, perhaps bowing to golfers' tired legs, St. Andrews reduced its length to eighteen holes from twenty-two. Three years later, James Durham played the course in ninety-four strokes, a record that stood for nearly a hundred years.

Meanwhile, across the Atlantic, the first golf club in the young United States was formed in Charleston, South Carolina, in 1786. That's the last time American wives saw their husbands on the weekends.

Golf exploded over the next fifty years, seeing the first women's tournament (1810 in Scotland), the first professional tournament (1819 at St. Andrews), and the first course outside Britain (1820 in Bangalore, India).

The first of thousands of golf instruction books, *The Golfing Manual by a Keen Hand,* was written by Henry Rarnie in 1857.

In 1858, St. Andrews announced new rules; the first said, "one round of the links or eighteen holes is reckoned to be a match." Other courses soon followed suit. That same year, Allan Robertson (known as the first professional golfer) was the first player to break eighty on the Old Course.

Around 1870, the first tee box was created. Previously, golfers had teed off from the previous green. Groundskeepers rejoiced.

The Royal Montreal Golf Club was formed in

1873 in Canada, and is the oldest continuously operating club in North America.

In 1874, George Herbert Walker was born. He later became president of the United States Golf Association and namesake of two future U.S. presidents. The Oakhurst Golf Club was founded in 1884 in Sulphur Springs, Virginia. Its first hole, now No. 1 at The Homestead resort, is considered the oldest surviving golf hole in America.

The U.S. Open is played for the first time in 1895, and the Chicago Golf Club opened the first eighteen-hole course in the U.S.

In 1908, Mrs. Gordon Robertson became the first female professional golfer.

In the next hundred years, golf would become a worldwide phenomenon, played by more than sixty million golfers, more than half of them in the United States.

BOBBY JONES

In his short and prolific career, Bobby Jones achieved great success in golf—and yet he never turned professional. Bobby was born on March 17, 1902, in Georgia. He was a child prodigy, reaching the third round of his first U.S. Amateur championship at age fourteen. With his flowing, rhythmical swing and quick playing style, Jones was a crowd pleaser as well as a great golfer and genuine hero. He captured the hearts of sports lovers by winning the Grand Slam of 1930, the U.S. and British Amateurs, and British and U.S. Opens. He was co-designer of the Augusta National Golf Club and a prolific writer on golf. He was also a mechanical engineer and a lawyer.

- *U.S. Amateur 1924, 1925, 1927, 1928, 1930*
- *British Amateur 1930*
- *U.S. Open 1923, 1926, 1929, 1930*
- *British Open 1926, 1927, 1930*
- *World Golf Hall of Fame 1974*

Sometimes the game of golf is just too difficult to endure with a golf club in your hands.

Bobby Jones (1902–1971)

EQUIPMENT

JOIN THE CLUB

Most golfers spend nearly as much time seeking the perfect club as they do using ones they have. Why are we so fixated on our clubs? Maybe to have something to blame when shots go awry!

The trouble that most of us find with the modern matched sets of clubs is that they don't really seem to know any more about the game than the old ones did.

Robert Browning (1812–1889)
Scottish author

The worst club in my bag is my brain.

Chris Perry (1961–)
Professional golfer

My clubs are well used, but unfortunately not used well.

Jack Burrell
Golf writer

Golf is a game whose aim is to hit a very small ball into an even smaller hole, with weapons singularly ill-designed for the purpose.

Winston Churchill (1874–1965)
British prime minister

If it really made sense to "let the club do the work," you'd just say, "Driver, wedge to the green, one-putt," and walk to the next tee.

Thomas Mulligan
Patron saint of do-overs

Golf is played with a number of striking implements more intricate in shape than those used in any form of recreation except dentistry.

E.V. Knox (1932-1949)
Magazine editor

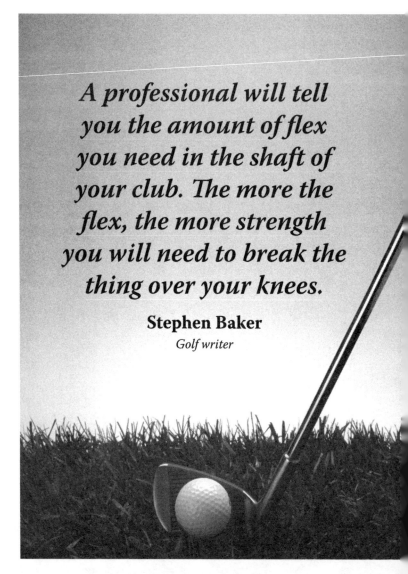

A professional will tell you the amount of flex you need in the shaft of your club. The more the flex, the more strength you will need to break the thing over your knees.

Stephen Baker

Golf writer

I may be the only golfer never to have broken a single putter, if you don't count the one I twisted into a loop and threw into a bush.

Thomas Boswell
Sportswriter, author

There's an old saying, "It's a poor craftsman who blames his tools." It's usually the player who misses those three-footers, not the putter.

Kathy Whitworth (1939–)
LPGA Hall of Fame golfer

Why am I using a new putter? Because the last one didn't float too well.

Craig Stadler (1953–)
Winner of the 1982 Masters

THE MYSTICAL ONE IRON

A good one iron shot is about
as easy to come by as an
understanding wife.

Dan Jenkins (1929–)
American author

Actually, the only time I ever took
out a one iron was to kill a tarantula.
And I took a seven to do that.

Jim Murray (1920–1998)
Sportwriter

When I'm on a golf course and it
starts to rain and lightning, I hold
up my one iron, 'cause I know
even God can't hit a one iron.

Lee Trevino (1939–)
Two-time winner of three majors:
U.S. Open, British Open, PGA

HISTORY OF GOLF GEAR

A Timeline

● 1452   Golf was already popular in Scotland, using simple hand-
          made wooden clubs and balls, or leather balls stuffed with
          wool or hair. Early records document the sale of golf balls.

● 1502   King James IV of Scotland takes up the game and buys a set
          of clubs from a bow-maker in Perth, the earliest documen-
          tation of selling golf gear.

● 1602   King James VI of Scotland has a set of golf clubs made
          especially for him, the first known occasion of clubs created
          for a particular golfer.

● 1603   James VI, apparently happy with his custom clubs, appoints
          William Mayne as Scotland's Royal Clubmaker, holding
          exclusive license throughout the kingdom.

● 1618   "Feathery" golf balls are introduced. Wet feathers stuffed
          tightly into a leather ball expanded as they dried, forming a
          solid sphere.

● 1642   A license was issued in Aberdeen, Scotland, to John Dick-
          son to make golf balls.

● 1687   The first book published about golf, *Thoughts On Golve* by
          Thomas Kincaid, included explanations of how golf clubs
          are made.

● 1743   Scotland exports golf equipment to the American colonies.

● 1780   Golf club makers begin using forged metal for the heads of
          niblicks (similar to today's wedges).

1826   Robert Forgan of Scotland imports hickory from America to manufacture shafts, replacing ash or hazel as the popular wood of choice.

1829   An inventor at the links at Musselburgh, Scotland, develops a hole-cutter with a 4.25-inch cutting blade. The size is eventually adopted as the standard for holes everywhere.

1832   Mowers manufactured especially for golf courses are introduced, though many courses still rely on sheep to keep the grass trimmed.

1848   The Reverend Roger Paterson introduces the gutta-percha or "guttie" golf ball, named for and made from the sap of a rubber tree. It receives enthusiastic response because it travels farther and costs less than the feathery.

1880   Manufacturers begin putting bumps and other protuberances on the surface of guttie balls, having discovered that the raised bumps make the ball travel farther.

1891   A metal-headed driver called the Currie MetalWood receives a patent in Britain. That same year, golf clubs with a steel shaft are advertised, and the 4.25-inch hole is set as the standard by the Royal and Ancient Golf Club of St. Andrews.

1985   The U.S.G.A. prohibits using a pool cue as a putter.

1898   Coburn Haskell designs and patents the first rubber-core golf ball. He calls it the Haskell ball.

● 1901   Walter Travis wins the U.S. Amateur using the Haskell ball, the first golfer to use it to win a major title. Almost everyone jumps on board the next year, when Laurie Auchterlonie wins the U.S. Open and Sandy Herd wins the British Open, both using Haskell balls.

● 1902   Irons with grooved faces are introduced.

● 1905   William Taylor receives a patent for the first dimple-patterned golf balls, in England.

● 1906   A golf ball with a rubber core filled with compressed air is introduced by Goodrich. The ball gives a peppy performance, but it has an unfortunate tendency to explode in warm weather—sometimes in the golfer's pocket. When Goodrich discontinues it, the Haskell again dominates.

● 1910   A forty-two-year era of conflicting golf rules begins when the Royal and Ancient Golf Club of St. Andrews prohibits using center-shafted putters. The U.S.G.A. says the center-shafted putter is allowed. The same year, Arthur F. Knight receives a patent for steel shafts.

● 1921   The allowable size and weight of a golf ball is limited by the Royal and Ancient Golf Club of St. Andrews.

● 1924   Steel-shafted golf clubs are approved by the USGA. Five years later, the R&A agrees.

● 1925   Irons with deep grooves are forbidden.

- 1931   The minimum golf ball size is raised by the USGA from 1.62 inches to 1.68 inches; maximum weight is decreased from 1.62 ounces to 1.55. The R&A does not agree. This "balloon ball" is hated by all, and eventually the USGA relents and raises the weight.

- 1932   The sand wedge is debuted by Gene Sarazen.

- 1942   Golf ball prices leap because of a worldwide shortage of rubber caused by World War II. Sam Snead finishes a four-day tourney with just one ball, but generally professional matches are halted. Soon, the U.S. government stops the manufacture of golf equipment until the war's end.

- 1951   The center-shafted putter is allowed around the world.

- 1972   The Top-Flite, the world's first two-piece ball, is introduced by Spalding.

- 1973   The first graphite shaft is created.

- 1979   The first metal woods are manufactured by Taylor Made.

- 1990   The R&A finally allows the 1.68-inch diameter ball after thirty-eight years, and golf rules are standardized for the first time in eighty years.

- 1991   Golfers see the first oversized metal woods, and Callaway Golf's Big Bertha soon becomes one of the biggest-selling golf clubs ever.

TRADITIONAL CLUB NAMES

Historic Scottish names for the clubs we currently have in our bag:

Driver: play club

2 wood: brassie

3 wood: spoon

4 wood: cleek

7 wood: ginty

2 iron: flat iron

5 iron: mashie

7 iron: mid-mashie

9 iron: niblick

HERE, CADDIE CADDIE

No one has a better poker face than a caddie. He's seen it all twice without laughing once.

If your caddie coaches you on the tee, "Hit it down the left side with a little draw," ignore him. All you do on the tee is try not to hit the caddie.

Jim Murray (1920–1998)
Sportswriter

After all these years, it's still embarrassing for me to play on the American golf tour. Like the time I asked my caddie for a sand wedge and he came back ten minutes later with a ham on rye.

Chi Chi Rodriguez (1935–)
Professional golfer

Many a golfer prefers a golf cart to a caddy because the cart cannot count, criticize, or laugh.

Author Unknown

My game is so bad I gotta hire three caddies—one to walk the left rough, one for the right, and one for the middle. And the one in the middle doesn't have much to do.

Dave Hill (1937-)
Professional golfer

Real golfers, no matter what the provocation, never strike a caddie with the driver. The sand wedge is far more effective.

Huxtable Pippey
Caddie

Bag rat: A caddie.

THE PLAID FAD

When you compare the golfer's "uniform" to those of other sports, it's understandable why golfers have never set new trends in the fashion industry.

"Play it as it lies" is one of the fundamental dictates of golf. The other is "Wear it if it clashes."

Henry Beard
Humorist

You can't call it a sport. You don't run, jump, you don't shoot, you don't pass. All you have to do is buy some clothes that don't match.

Steve Sax (1960–)
Major league baseball player

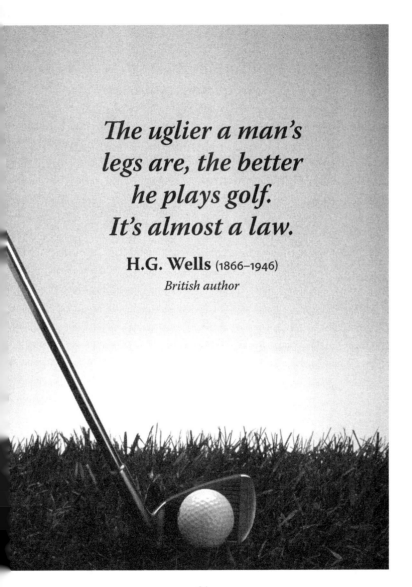

The uglier a man's legs are, the better he plays golf. It's almost a law.

H.G. Wells (1866–1946)

British author

Here's a simple way to abolish golf's elitist and exclusionary image and make it a truly all-American sport: ditch that fifties-Republican-martini-drinker's green Brooks Brothers-style sport jacket and make the winner of the Masters slip on something in, say, black leather with plenty of metal studs.

Bruce McCall
Writer, artist

I'd give up golf if I didn't have so many sweaters.

Bob Hope (1903–2003)
Comedian

I don't like the way most people dress on the golf course. I think it's pretty bland, pretty boring.

Ian Poulter (1976–)
Professional golfer

Although golf was originally restricted
to wealthy, overweight Protestants,
today it's open to anybody
who owns hideous clothing.

Dave Barry (1947–)
Pulitzer Prize-winning humorist

Baffling late-life discovery: golfers
wear those awful clothes on purpose.

Herb Caen (1916–1997)
Columnist

Nobody asked how you looked,
just what you shot.

Sam Snead (1912–2003)
*PGA Tour career victory
leader with eighty-one wins*

zucchini: Rough.

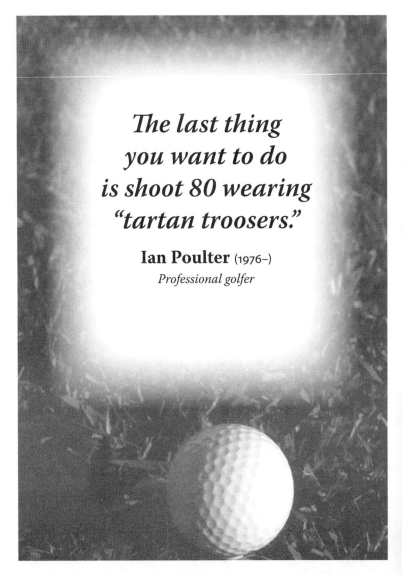

The last thing you want to do is shoot 80 wearing "tartan troosers."

Ian Poulter (1976–)

Professional golfer

BETTER GOLF

You can get plenty of advice from everyone. It's knowing which to follow that makes you a better golfer.

Only one golfer in a thousand grips the club lightly enough.

Johnny Miller (1947–)
Professional golfer

The secret of good golf is to hit the ball hard, straight, and not too often.

Author Unknown

Always count your blessings. Be thankful you are able to be out on a beautiful course. Most people in the world don't have that opportunity.

Fred Couples (1959–)
Winner of the 1992 Masters

A golfer's diet: live on greens
as much as possible.

Author Unknown

You must work very hard
to become a natural golfer.

Gary Player (1936–)
Professional golfer

It is nothing new or original to say
that golf is played one stroke at a time.
But it took me many years to realize it.

Bobby Jones (1902–1971)
*Winner of four U.S. Opens, five U.S. Amateurs,
three British Opens; founder of the Masters*

Most golfers prepare for
disaster. A good golfer
prepares for success.

Bob Toski (1927–)
Professional golfer, instructor

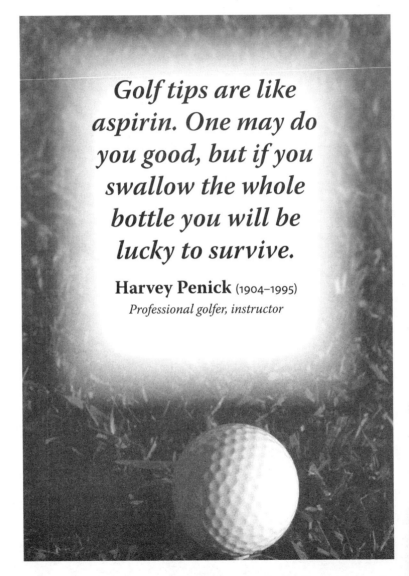

Golf tips are like aspirin. One may do you good, but if you swallow the whole bottle you will be lucky to survive.

Harvey Penick (1904–1995)
Professional golfer, instructor

You've just got one problem. You stand too close to the ball after you've hit it.

Sam Snead (1912–2003)
*PGA Tour career victory
leader with eighty-one wins*

There are three ways of
learning golf: by study,
which is the most wearisome;
by imitation, which is the most
fallacious; and by experience,
which is the most bitter.

Robert Browning (1812–1889)
Scottish author

The person I fear most in the
last two rounds is myself.

Tom Watson (1949–)
*Winner of five British Opens,
two Masters, U.S. Open*

Hit 'em hard. They'll land somewhere.

Stewart Maiden
Bobby Jones's golf teacher

A golf ball is like a clock. Always
hit it at six o'clock and make it go
toward twelve o'clock. But make sure
you're in the same time zone.

Chi Chi Rodriguez (1935–)
Professional golfer

Imagine the ball has little
legs, and chop them off.

Henry Cotton (1907–1997)
Winner of three British Opens

Don't play too much golf.
Two rounds a day are plenty.

Harry Vardon (1870–1939)
Winner of six British Opens, U.S. Open

Don't let the bad shots get to you.
Don't let yourself become angry. The
true scramblers are thick-skinned.
They always beat the whiners.

Paul Runyan (1909–2002)
Winner of two PGA championships

No golfer ever gets so consistently good
that he can't use some constructive
advice. No matter how many
trophies he may win, he can't analyze
and remedy his own faults.

Byron Nelson (1912–)
Winner of two PGA championships, U.S. Open

That little ball won't move until
you hit it, and there's nothing you
can do for it after it has gone.

Babe Didrikson Zaharias (1914–1956)
Winner of eighty-two tournaments

If you drink, don't drive.
Don't even putt.

Dean Martin (1917–1995)
Singer, actor

If you break one hundred,
watch your golf. If you break
eighty, watch your business.

Joey Adams (1911–1999)
Comedian

Keep close count of
your nickels and dimes,
stay away from whiskey, and
never concede a putt.

Sam Snead (1912–2003)
*PGA Tour career victory
leader with eighty-one wins*

Don't be in such a hurry.
That little white ball isn't
going to run away from you.

Patty Berg (1918–)
*Professional golfer, founding
member of LPGA*

To help your concentration,
don't take too much time.

Pam Barnett (1944–)
Professional golfer

When it's breezy, hit it easy.

Davis Love, Jr. (1935–1988)
Golf instructor

Don't be too proud to take
lessons. I'm not.

Jack Nicklaus (1940–)
*All-time leader in major tournament
wins with twenty, including six Masters*

HEAD'S UP: HEAD DOWN

On the underside of the roof of a golf cart:
You're looking up.
That's your problem.

Author Unknown

Nobody ever looked up
and saw a good shot.

Don Herold (1889-1966)
Author, humorist

There are two things you can do with
your head down: play golf and pray.

Lee Trevino (1939–)
Two-time winner of three majors:
U.S. Open, British Open, PGA

The worst advice in golf is,
"Keep your head down."

Patty Sheehan (1956–)
Professional golfer

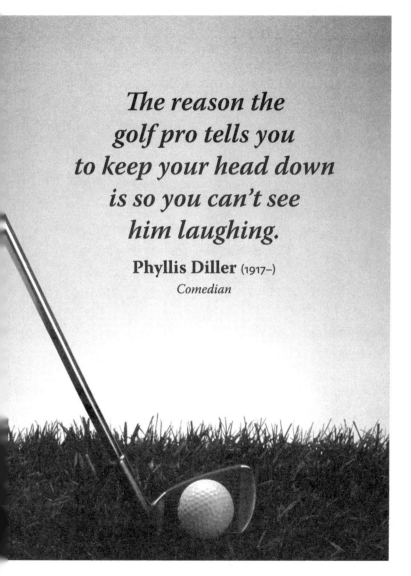

The reason the golf pro tells you to keep your head down is so you can't see him laughing.

Phyllis Diller (1917–)
Comedian

HOLE-IN-ONE

It's what every golfer lives for . . . a sweet swing, a perfect line, and the ball finds the cup like it has eyes. Write down a "1" and head for the next tee.

Man blames fate for other
accidents but feels
personally responsible
for a hole-in-one.

Martha Beckman
Author

A hole-in-one is amazing when
you think of the different
universes this white mass of
molecules has to pass through
on its way to the hole.

Mac O'Grady (1941–)
Golf instructor

Hitting a tree in West Texas is stranger than getting a hole-in-one.

Mancil Davis
Hole-in-one record holder

I played golf . . . I did not get a hole-in-one, but I did hit a guy. That's way more satisfying.

Mitch Hedberg (1968–2005)
American comedian

Hole-in-one: an occurrence in which a ball is hit directly from the tee into the hole in a single shot by a golfer playing alone.

Henry Beard
Humorist

My golf is improving. Yesterday I hit the ball in one!

Jane Swan (1943–)
Australian writer

History of the Hole-in-One

1868   Young Tom Morris scores the first recorded hole-in-one.

1952   The National Hole-in-One Clearing House is established by *Golf Digest*.

1962   Dr. Joseph Boydstone records eleven aces in one calendar year. Three were recorded in one round, at Bakersfield Country Club in California.

1964   Norman Manley, an amateur from Long Beach, Calif., scores holes-in-one on two successive par-fours at Del Valley Country Club in California. It is the first and only time this feat has been accomplished.

1968   Tommy Moore, age six years one month, one week, becomes the youngest player to score a hole-in-one. Moore also becomes, in 1975, the youngest player ever to score a double-eagle.

PLAYING THOSE MIND GAMES

The mind messes up more shots
than the body.

Tommy Bolt (1918–)
Winner of the 1958 U.S. Open

One hundred years of experience has
demonstrated that the game is temporary
insanity practiced in a pasture.

Dave Kindred
Sportswriter

I'm about five inches from being an
outstanding golfer. That's the distance
my left ear is from my right.

Ben Crenshaw (1952–)
Winner of two Masters

Let's face it, ninety-five percent of this
game is mental. A guy plays lousy golf,
he doesn't need a pro, he needs a shrink.

Tom Murphy
Course designer

THE SWING'S THE THING

Head down. Elbows in. Arm straight. Weight shifted. Knees bent. Feet parallel. Eye on the ball. There's a lot to think about. Maybe that's why the swing is the greatest challenge in golf.

The golf swing is like a suitcase into which we are trying to pack one too many things.

John Updike (1932–)
American author

My swing is so bad I look like a caveman killing his lunch.

Lee Trevino (1939–)
Two-time winner of three majors: U.S. Open, British Open, PGA

Swing hard in case you hit it.

Dan Marino (1961–)
Professional football player

A physicist can describe the perfect golf swing and write it down in scientific language, but the smart golfer doesn't read it. The smart golfer gives it to his opponent to contemplate.

Dr. Fran Pirozzollo
Sports psychologist

There is no movement in the golf swing so difficult that it cannot be made even more difficult by careful study and diligent practice.

Thomas Mulligan
Patron saint of do-overs

chicken wing: The flying elbow or bent elbow, on your downswing or backswing. "All my life, I fought the dreaded chicken wing."

John Daly certainly gives it a good
hit, doesn't he? My Sunday best is a
Wednesday afternoon compared to him.

Nick Faldo (1957–)
Winner of three Masters, three British Opens

Rhythm is best expressed in
any swing directed at a cigar
stump or a dandelion head.

Grantland Rice (1880–1954)
Sportswriter

The swing is never learned.
It's remembered.

Bagger Vance
Title character of The Legend of Bagger Vance

in between swings: In between your old
swing and a new swing you are still learning.

A golf swing is a collection
of corrected mistakes.

Carol Mann (1941–)
Hall of Fame golfer

We were always taught to swing
slow with good tempo. But you
have to have some acceleration
throughout the swing. I think
that's where a lot of women go
wrong. They should try to whack
it a few times and see what happens.

Helen Alfredsson (1965–)
Professional golfer

Because golf exposes the flaws of the
human swing—a basically simple
maneuver—it causes more self-torture
than any game short of Russian roulette.

Grantland Rice (1880–1954)
Sportswriter

Note pinned to Vijay Singh's golf bag
when he won the 2000 Masters:
Papa, trust your swing.

Qass Singh (1990–)
Daughter of professional golfer

As far as swing and techniques
are concerned, I don't know
diddly squat. When I'm playing
well, I don't even take aim.

Fred Couples (1959–)
Winner of the 1992 Masters

Dividing the swing into
its parts is like dissecting a cat.
You'll have blood and guts and
bones all over the place. But
you won't have a cat.

Ernest Jones
Golf instructor

On why he tees the ball up high:
Through years of experience I
have found that air offers less
resistance than dirt.

Jack Nicklaus (1940–)
*All-time leader in major tournament
wins with twenty, including six Masters*

The right way to play golf is to go
up and hit the bloody thing.

George Duncan (1883–?)
Professional golfer

There are two things you can
learn by stopping your backswing
at the top and checking the position
of your hands; how many hands
you have, and which one
is wearing the glove.

Thomas Mulligan
Patron saint of do-overs

The best place to refine your swing is, of course, on the practice range. You will have an opportunity to make the same mistakes over and over again so that you no longer have to think about them, and they become part of your game.

Stephen Baker
Golf writer

Reverse every natural instinct and do the opposite of what you are inclined to do, and you will probably come very close to having a perfect golf swing.

Ben Hogan (1912–1997)
Winner of two Masters, four U.S. Opens, British Open

to baff: To hit or scuff the ground behind the ball. Not necessarily bad golf. If you baff the ball right, without too much ground, you hit the ball clean.

You swing your best when you have the fewest things to think about.

Bobby Jones (1902–1971)

Winner of four U.S. Opens, five U.S. Amateurs, three British Opens; founder of the Masters

The best stroked putt in a
lifetime does not bring the
aesthetic satisfaction of a
perfectly hit wood or iron shot.
There is nothing to match the
whoosh and soar, the almost
magical flight of a beautifully
hit drive or five-iron.

Al Barkow
Golf writer

Everybody has two swings—a
beautiful practice swing and the
choked-up one with which they
hit the ball. So it wouldn't do
either of us a damned bit of good
to look at your practice swing.

Ed Furgol (1918–1997)
Professional golfer

If I hit it right, it's a slice.
If I hit it left, it's a hook.
If I hit it straight, it's a miracle.

Author Unknown

I'm not saying my golf game went bad, but if I grew tomatoes, they'd come up sliced.

Lee Trevino (1939–)
Two-time winner of three majors:
U.S. Open, British Open, PGA

Selecting a stroke is like selecting a wife. To each his own.

Ben Hogan (1912–1997)
Winner of two Masters, four U.S. Opens, British Open

It's not just enough to swing at the ball. You've got to loosen your girdle and really let the ball have it.

Babe Didrikson Zaharias (1914–1956)
Winner of eighty-two tournaments

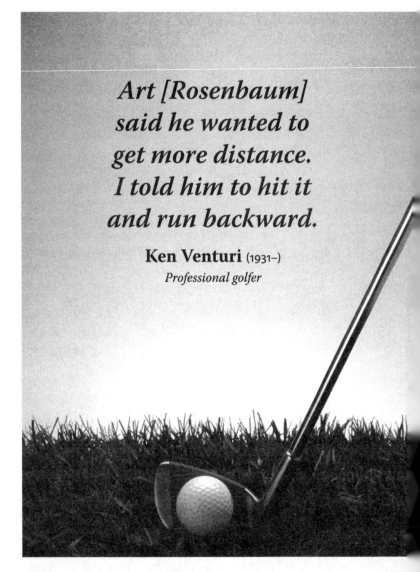

Art [Rosenbaum] said he wanted to get more distance. I told him to hit it and run backward.

Ken Venturi (1931–)
Professional golfer

ANNIKA SORENSTAM

Annika Sorenstam was born in Sweden on October 9, 1970, and she didn't take up golf until she was twelve, focusing on tennis until that time. She approaches golf with an intense desire to win. Determined in her study, practice, and workouts, she regularly completes over seven hundred sit-ups a day. In 1990, Annika began the University of Arizona, where she was an All-American golfer in 1991 and 1992. She competed on the European tour before joining the LPGA Tour in 1994. Voted the Associated Press Female Athlete of the Year in 2003, she was also inducted into the World Golf Hall of Fame.

- *LPGA Championship 2003, 2004*
- *Women's British Open 2003*
- *U.S. Women's Open Championship 1995, 1996*

To play well you have to have balance in your life. If you play golf long enough you'll learn that life is more than golf.

Annika Sorenstam (1970–)

PUTT . . . PUTT . . . PUTT . . .

Somehow it's a lot easier to knock a ball three hundred yards than to putt it eighteen inches. This is one of the greatest mysteries of golf.

Find a man with both feet
firmly on the ground and
you've found a man about to
make a difficult putt.

Fletcher Knebel (1911–1993)
American author

These greens are so fast
I have to hold my putter
over the ball and hit it
with the shadow.

Sam Snead (1912–2003)
*PGA Tour career victory
leader with eighty-one wins*

On his putting: It's so bad I could
putt off a tabletop and still leave
the ball halfway down the leg.

J.C. Snead (1940–)
Professional golfer

The game of golf would lose
a great deal if croquet mallets
and billiard cues were allowed
on the putting green.

Ernest Hemingway (1899–1961)
American author

There are no points for style
when it comes to putting. It's
getting the ball in the cup
that counts.

Brian Swarbrick
Golf writer

A "gimme" can best be defined as
an agreement between two golfers,
neither of whom can putt very well.

Author Unknown

Asked if he had any uphill putts:
Yeah, after each of my downhill putts.

Homero Blancas (1938–)
Professional golfer

Missing a short putt does not
mean you have to hit your
next drive out of bounds.

Henry Cotton (1907–1997)
Winner of three British Opens

The better you putt,
the bolder you play.

Don January (1929–)
Professional golfer

Putts get real difficult the day
they hand out the money.

Lee Trevino (1939–)
Two-time winner of three majors:
U.S. Open, British Open, PGA

I don't fear death . . .
but I sure do hate those
three footers for par.

Chi Chi Rodriguez (1935–)
Professional golfer

I may be the only golfer
never to have broken a
single putter, if you don't count
the one I twisted into a loop
and threw into a bush.

Thomas Boswell
Sportswriter, author

Around a clubhouse they'll tell you
even God has to practise his putting.
In fact, even Nicklaus does.

Jim Murray (1920–1998)
Sportswriter

While, on the whole, playing
through the green is the part most
trying to the temper, putting is that
most trying to the nerves. There is
always the hope that a bad drive
may be redeemed by a fine approach
shot, or that a "foozle" with the brassy
may be balanced by some brilliant
performance with the iron. But
when the stage of putting-out
has been reached no further
illusions are possible.

A.J. Balfour (1848–1930)
British prime minister

Hitting a golf ball and putting have nothing in common. They're two different games. You work all your life to perfect a repeating swing that will get you to the greens, and then you have to try to do something that is totally unrelated. There shouldn't be any cups, just flag sticks. And then the man who hit the most fairways and greens and got closest to the pins would be the tournament winner.

Ben Hogan (1912–1997)
Winner of two Masters, four U.S. Opens, British Open

A good player who is a great putter is a match for any golfer. A great hitter who cannot putt is a match for no one.

Ben Sayers (1857–1924)
British golfer, ball manufacturer, and course designer

I enjoy the oohs! and aahs! from the gallery when I hit my drives. But I'm getting pretty tired of the awws! and uhhs! when I miss the putt.

John Daly (1966–)
Winner of the 1995 British Open

The next time you see a good player stalking backward and forwards on the green, do not be led away by the idea that he is especially painstaking, but rather pity him for a nervous individual who is putting off the evil moment as long as he possibly can.

Ted Ray
Early twentieth-century British champion

Happiness is a long walk with a putter.

Greg Norman (1955–)
Winner of two British Opens

*A man who can
putt is a match
for anyone.*

Willie Park (1834–1903)
*Won four British Opens,
including the first*

A tap-in is a putt that is short
enough to be missed one-handed.

Henry Beard
Humorist

Love and putting are mysteries
for the philosopher to solve. Both
subjects are beyond golfers.

Tommy Armour (1895–1968)
*Winner of the U.S. Open, British
Open, PGA championship*

The devoted golfer is an anguished
soul who has learned a lot about
putting, just as an avalanche victim
has learned a lot about snow.

Dan Jenkins (1929–)
American author

the ball is afraid of the dark: The putt won't go in.

When a putter is waiting his turn to hole out a putt of one or two feet in length, on which the match hangs at the last hole, it is of vital importance that he think of nothing. At this supreme moment he ought to fill his mind with vacancy. He must not even allow himself the consolation of religion.

Sir Walter Simpson
Nineteenth-century Scottish philosopher

When I putt, my emotions collide like tectonic plates. It's left my memory circuits full of scars that won't heal.

Mac O'Grady (1941–)
Golf instructor

You drive for show but putt for dough.

Bobby Locke (1918–1969)
Winner of four British Opens

BEN HOGAN

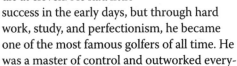

Seldom seen without the visor of his white cap pulled over his face, Ben Hogan won nine of the sixteen majors he competed in between 1946 and 1953. Born in Texas on August 13, 1912, Ben began to caddie at eleven. He had little success in the early days, but through hard work, study, and perfectionism, he became one of the most famous golfers of all time. He was a master of control and outworked everyone. He had a tendency to hook, and didn't reach the top until he found his "secret," a backswing change that allowed him to play a powerful fade. An automobile accident in 1949 caused him much pain, but afterwards he played some of his best golf.

- *Masters 1951, 1953*
- *U.S. Open 1948, 1950, 1951, 1953*
- *British Open 1953*
- *PGA 1946, 1948*
- *World Golf Hall of Fame 1974*

The only thing a golfer needs
is more daylight.

Ben Hogan (1912–1997)

THE
LIGHTER SIDE

THE LIGHTER SIDE

Golfers are known for their sense of humor—it's a case of laughing to keep from crying.

I don't think I'll live long
enough to shoot my age. I'm
lucky to shoot my weight.

Bruce Lansky
American author

I'll shoot my age if I have to live
to be a hundred and five.

Bob Hope (1903–2003)
Comedian

I found out that all the important
lessons of life are contained in the
three rules for achieving a perfect
golf swing: 1.Keep your head down. 2.
Follow through. 3. Be born with money

P.J. O'Rourke (1941–)
Satirist

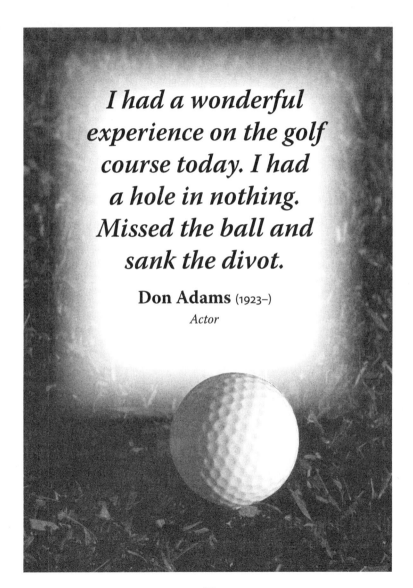

I had a wonderful experience on the golf course today. I had a hole in nothing. Missed the ball and sank the divot.

Don Adams (1923–)

Actor

Columbus went around the world
in 1492. That isn't a lot of strokes
when you consider the course.

Lee Trevino (1939–)
Two-time winner of three majors:
U.S. Open, British Open, PGA

Show me a man who is a good
loser and I'll show you a man who
is playing golf with his boss.

Jim Murray (1920–1998)
Sportswriter

On how he was one under for the day:
One under a tree,
one under a bush,
one under the water.

Lee Trevino (1939–)
Two-time winner of three majors:
U.S. Open, British Open, PGA

If you think it's hard to meet new people, try picking up the wrong golf ball.

Jack Lemmon (1925–2001)
Actor

Obviously a deer on the fairway has seen you tee off before and knows that the safest place to be when you play is right down the middle.

Jackie Gleason (1916–1987)
Actor, comedian

While playing golf today I hit two good balls. I stepped on a rake.

Henny Youngman (1906–1998)
Comedian

I owe a lot to my parents, especially my mother and my father.

Greg Norman (1955–)
Winner of two British Opens

I played golf with a priest
the other day. He shot
par-par-par-par-par.
Finally I said to him,
"Father, if you're playing golf
like this you haven't been
saving many souls lately."

Sam Snead (1912–2003)
*PGA Tour career victory
leader with eighty-one wins*

Golf! You hit down to
make the ball go up.
You swing left and the
ball goes right. The
lowest score wins. And
on top of that, the winner
buys the drinks.

Author Unknown

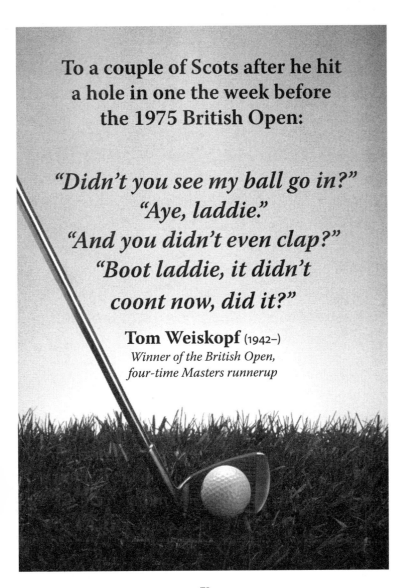

To a couple of Scots after he hit
a hole in one the week before
the 1975 British Open:

"Didn't you see my ball go in?"
"Aye, laddie."
"And you didn't even clap?"
"Boot laddie, it didn't
coont now, did it?"

Tom Weiskopf (1942–)
Winner of the British Open,
four-time Masters runnerup

THEY JUST DON'T GET IT

*A*s popular as golf is around the world, some people just don't like it.

Golf seems to me an arduous way to go for a walk. I prefer to take the dogs out.

Princess Anne (1950–)
Daughter of Queen Elizabeth

Give me the fresh air, a beautiful partner, and a nice round of golf, and you can keep the fresh air and the round of golf.

Jack Benny (1894–1974)
Comedian

He enjoys that perfect peace, that peace beyond all understanding, which comes at its maximum only to the man who has given up golf.

P.G. Wodehouse (1881–1975)
British author

Golf is a good walk spoiled.

Mark Twain (1835–1910)
Author

I regard golf as an expensive
way of playing marbles.

G.K. Chesterton (1874–1936)
English author

If I had my way, any man guilty of golf
would be barred from any public office
in the United States and the families
of the breed would be shipped off to
the white slave corrals of Argentina.

H.L. Mencken (1880–1956)
Journalist

Any game where a man sixty can
beat a man thirty ain't no game.

Burt Shotten (1884–1962)
Professional baseball player

CHI CHI RODRIGUEZ

Known as one of the great showmen in sports history, Chi Chi was born on October 23, 1935, in Puerto Rico. His family was poor and Chi Chi saw athletics as a way to make a better life. He boxed as a young man and was a baseball pitcher. He became a caddie at the age of eight, and had an aptitude for golf. He began playing after two years in the Army. A flamboyant player, he would often wave his putter like a sword after making a putt. He has been very successful on the Senior PGA Tour. His youth foundation in Clearwater, Florida, helps six hundred children from low-income families a year.

● *World Golf Hall of Fame 1992*

I never pray to God to make a putt. I pray to God to help me react good if I miss a putt.

Chi Chi Rodriguez (1935–)

PLAYERS

IT HURTS SO GOOD

When you see their misery, it's hard to remember golfers do it on purpose.

Next to sunburn, a visit to the dentist, or a wasp sting on the privates, nothing gives a man more masochistic satisfaction than a round of golf.

Archie Compston
British golf pioneer

Golf is essentially an exercise in masochism conducted out-of-doors.

Paul O'Neil (1953–)
Professional baseball player

Yes, it is a cruel game, one in which the primitive instincts of man are given full play, and the difference between golf and fisticuffs is that in one the pain is of the mind and in the other it is of the body.

Henry Leach
English author

Golf is the cruelest of sports. Like life, it's unfair. It's a harlot. A trollop. It leads you on. It never lives up to its promises. . . . It's a boulevard of broken dreams. It plays with men. And runs off with the butcher.

Jim Murray (1920–1998)
Sportswriter

Golf is an open exhibition of overweening ambition, courage deflated by stupidity, skill scoured by a whiff of arrogance.

Alistair Cooke (1908–2004)
British journalist

Golf is not a game, it's bondage. It was obviously devised by a man torn with guilt, eager to atone for his sins.

Jim Murray (1920–1998)
Sportswriter

Golf is good for the soul. You get so mad at yourself you forget to hate your enemies.

Will Rogers (1879–1935)

Humorist

Eighteen holes of match or medal play will teach you more about your foe than will eighteen years of dealing with him across a desk.

Grantland Rice (1880–1954)
Sportswriter

I look into their eyes, shake their hand, pat their back, and wish them luck, but I am thinking, "I am going to bury you."

Seve Ballesteros (1957–)
Winner of three British Opens, two Masters

If your opponent is playing several shots in vain attempts to extricate himself from a bunker, do not stand near him and audibly count his strokes. It would be justifiable homicide if he wound up his pitiable exhibition by applying his niblick to your head.

Harry Vardon (1870–1939)
Winner of six British Opens, U.S. Open

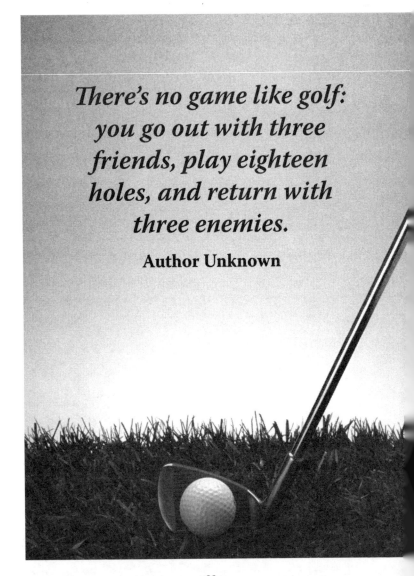

There's no game like golf: you go out with three friends, play eighteen holes, and return with three enemies.

Author Unknown

MAGNIFICENT OBSESSION

Watch golf. Play golf. Think about golf. Repeat. A golfer will tell you that sometimes obsession is a good thing.

The ardent golfer would play
Mount Everest if somebody
put a flagstick on top.

Pete Dye
Course architect

I'm a golfaholic, no question
about that. Counseling wouldn't
help me. They'd have to put me
in prison, and then I'd talk the
warden into building a hole or
two and teach him how to play.

Lee Trevino (1939–)
Two-time winner of three majors:
U.S. Open, British Open, PGA

If you find you do not mind playing golf in the rain, the snow, even during a hurricane, here's a valuable tip: Your life is in trouble.

Author Unknown

Fame is addictive. Money is addictive. Attention is addictive. But golf is second to none.

Marc Anthony (1968–)
Latin pop singer

When you fall in love with golf, you seldom fall easy. It's obsession at first sight.

Thomas Boswell
Sportswriter, author

Like other forms of compulsive behavior, for true golfaholics even nine holes are more then they should attempt, yet eighteen holes are not enough to satisfy their insatiable craving for humiliation and self-abuse.

Mark Oman

Golf author, humorist

I played golf every day of my life nearly until a few years ago, except Sundays, and I gave it up. I'm not going to tell you why I gave it up—but there wasn't enough exercise to me, and there's not enough money to pay those fees. I almost went to the government for a loan.

Billy Graham (1918–)
Evangelist

Once bitten, it is akin to having your neck punctured in Transylvania— there is no known antidote.

Martin Johnson
Sportswriter

Golf, like the measles, should be caught young, for, if postponed to riper years, the results may be serious.

P.G. Wodehouse (1881–1975)
British author

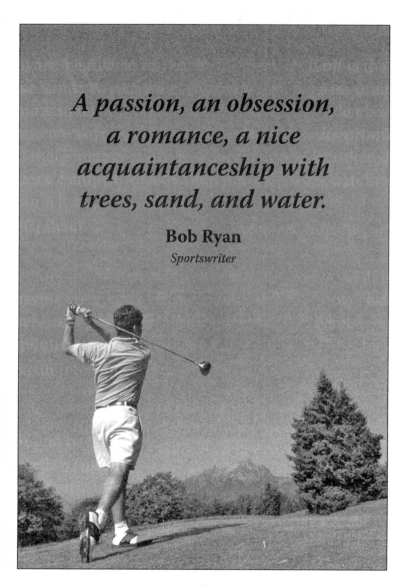

A passion, an obsession, a romance, a nice acquaintanceship with trees, sand, and water.

Bob Ryan
Sportswriter

GOLF WIDOWS

Many women end up wishing their husbands had a girlfriend instead of a golf game. At least they'd get to see their men once in a while.

When I die, bury me on the golf course so my husband will visit.

Author Unknown

Many men are more faithful to their golf partners than to their wives and have stuck with them longer.

John Updike (1932–)
American author

divorce channel: The Golf Channel proves to the dismay of wives everywhere, that men really will watch golf twenty-four hours a day..

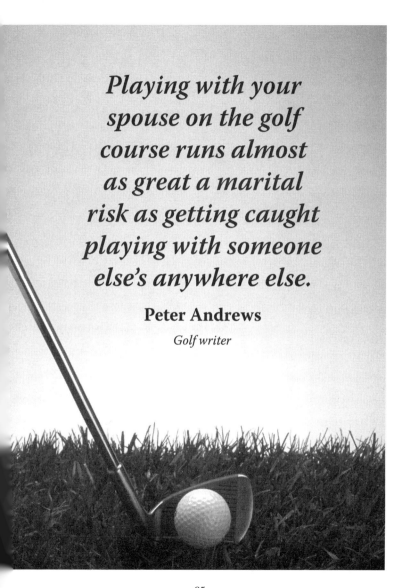

Playing with your spouse on the golf course runs almost as great a marital risk as getting caught playing with someone else's anywhere else.

Peter Andrews

Golf writer

"After all, golf is only a game," said Millicent. Women say these things without thinking. It does not mean that there is a kink in their character. They simply don't realize what they are saying.

P.G. Wodehouse (1881–1975)
British author

The place of the father in the modern suburban family is a very small one, particularly if he plays golf.

Bertrand Russell (1872–1970)
Philosopher, writer

Shall the married man play golf? This admits of no argument. Certainly. Of all the plagues to a woman in the house is a man during the day.

Dr. Proudfoot
Nineteenth-century physician

Golf is played by twenty million
mature American men whose wives
think they are out having fun.

Jim Bishop (1907-1987)
Journalist

A golfer needs a loving wife to
whom he can describe the day's
play through the long evening.

P.G. Wodehouse (1881–1975)
British author

The only really unplayable lie I can
think of is when you're supposed
to be playing golf and come home
with lipstick on your collar.

Arnold Palmer (1929–)
*Sixty wins on PGA Tour, including four
Masters, two British Opens, U.S. Open*

Golf is like marriage: If you take yourself too seriously it won't work . . . and both are expensive.

Author Unknown

NANCY LOPEZ

The calm attitude and great skill of Nancy Lopez have made her one of the LPGA's brightest stars. Nancy was born in California on January 6, 1957. Her father introduced her to golf at age eight, and she won the New Mexico Women's Amateur Championship at twelve. She was largely self-taught and her unconventional loopy swing was criticized, but she became a competitive player with a very accurate putting touch. She turned pro in 1977 and focused attention on women's golf in 1978 when she won five LPGA events in succession.

- *LPGA 1978, 1985, 1989*
- *World Golf Hall of Fame 1989*

My swing is no uglier than Arnold Palmer's, and it's the same swing every time.

Nancy Lopez (1957–)

PRESIDENTS ALWAYS WIN

Republican or Democrat, elected by landslide or appointed, the most powerful man in the world is frequently humbled by the little white ball.

That does look like very good exercise.
But what is the little white ball for?

Ulysses S. Grant (1822–1885)
18th President of the United States

One lesson you had better learn
if you want to be in politics is
that you never go out on a golf
course and beat the President.

Lyndon B. Johnson (1908–1973)
36th President of the United States

I know I am getting better at golf
because I am hitting fewer spectators.

Gerald Ford (1913–)
38th President of the United States

How has retirement affected
my golf game? A lot more
people beat me now.

Dwight D. Eisenhower (1890–1969)
34th President of the United States

Golf is an ineffectual attempt to
put an elusive ball into an
obscure hole with implements
ill-adapted to the purpose.

Woodrow Wilson (1856–1924)
28th President of the United States

I would like to deny all allegations
by Bob Hope that during my last
game of golf, I hit an eagle,
a birdie, an elk, and a moose.

Gerald Ford (1913–)
38th President of the United States

The problem with golf is I have to
deal with a humiliation factor.

George W. Bush (1946–)
43rd President of the United States

The great thing about
this game is that the
bad days are wonderful.

Bill Clinton (1946–)
42nd President of the United States

It is true that my predecessor
did not object as I do to pictures
of one's golf skill in action. But
neither, on the other hand, did he
ever bean a Secret Service man.

John F. Kennedy (1917–1963)
35th President of the United States

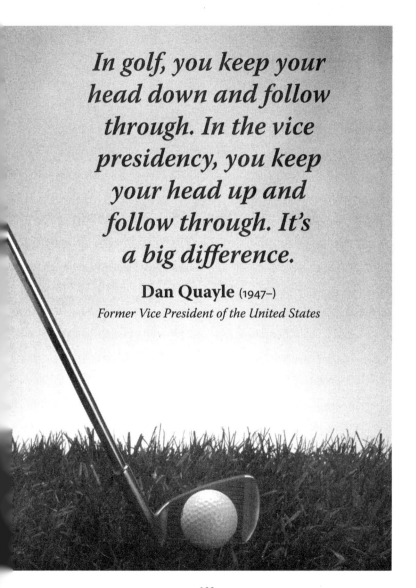

In golf, you keep your head down and follow through. In the vice presidency, you keep your head up and follow through. It's a big difference.

Dan Quayle (1947–)
Former Vice President of the United States

*!#@?/#

They just seem to go together sometimes. A bad swing and [expletive deleted]. A missed putt and [expletive deleted]. You hear the most creative language on the golf course.

They call it golf because all the other four-letter words were taken.

Raymond Floyd (1942–)
Winner of two PGA championships,
Masters, U.S. Open

He's nice to people 'n animals, but you oughta hear him talkin' to a golf ball!

Dennis the Menace

I just hope I don't have to explain all the times I've used His name in vain when I get up there.

Bob Hope (1903–2003)
Comedian

I used to go to the driving range
to practice driving without slicing.
Now I go to the driving range to
practice slicing without swearing.

Bruce Lansky
American author

If profanity had an influence on the
flight of the ball, the game of golf
would be played far better than it is.

Horace G. Hutchinson (1859–1932)
Golf writer

The number of shots taken by an
opponent who is out of sight is
equal to the square root of the
sum of the number of curses heard
plus the number of swishes.

Michael Green
Author

TOMMY BOLT

Tommy Bolt is known almost as much for his temper and for throwing his clubs as for his excellent golfing skills. Caddying at the local country club was Tommy's introduction to golf. He pursued the game when he could afford to, and made his living as a carpenter. He joined the PGA tour when he was thirty-four, and has been involved in golf as a player, a pro at a golf club, and an operator of a driving range. Known as "Terrible Tommy" for his temper, Bolt was thrilled to be elected to the World Golf Hall of Fame in 2002.

● *U.S. Open Championship 1958*

> Golf is a game where guts and blind devotion will always net you absolutely nothing but an ulcer.

Tommy Bolt (1918–)

Always throw your clubs
ahead of you. That way you
don't have to waste energy
going back to pick them up.

Tommy Bolt (1918–)
Winner of the 1958 U.S. Open

I've thrown or broken a few
clubs in my day. In fact,
I guess at one time or another
I probably held distance records
for every club in the bag.

Tommy Bolt (1918–)
Winner of the 1958 U.S. Open

Never break your putter and
your driver in the same
round or you're dead.

Tommy Bolt (1918–)
Winner of the 1958 U.S. Open

*G*olfers have and unusual relationship with the truth. They say, "Play it as it lays," but too often they mean "lies."

Golf makes liars out of honest
men, cheats out of altruists,
cowards out of brave men
and fools out of everybody.

Milton Gross (1912-1973)
American author

If there is any larceny in a
man, golf will bring it out.

Paul Gallico (1897–1976)
Sportswriter, novelist

Golf is the hardest game in the world
to play, and the easiest to cheat at.

Ben Hogan (1912–1997)
Winner of two Masters, four U.S. Opens, British Open

He who has the fastest golf
cart never has a bad lie.

Mickey Mantle (1931–1995)
Hall of Fame baseball player

Golf is a game in which you yell "fore,"
shoot six, and write down five.

Paul Harvey (1918–)
Broadcaster

Golf is a game in which the ball
lies poorly and the players well.

Art Rosenbaum (1912–2003)
Sportswriter

The best wood in most
amateurs' bags is the pencil.

Author Unknown

Golf is based on honesty:
Where else would you admit
to a seven on a par three?

Jimmy Demaret (1910–)
First player to win the Masters three times

If you pick up a golfer and
hold him close to your ear, like
a conch shell, and listen,
you will hear an alibi.

Fred Beck
Humorist

Isn't it fun to go out on the
course and lie in the sun?

Bob Hope (1903–2003)
Comedian

Nothing increases your golf
score like witnesses.

Author Unknown

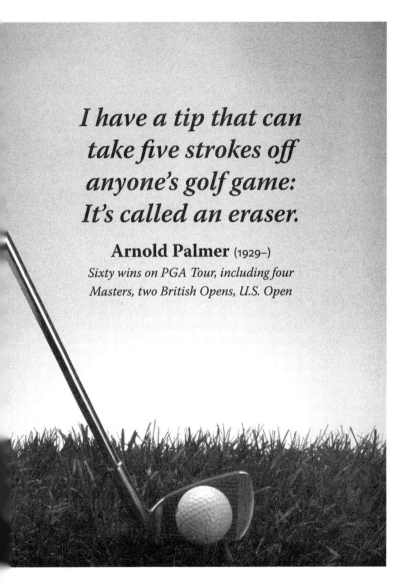

I have a tip that can take five strokes off anyone's golf game: It's called an eraser.

Arnold Palmer (1929–)
Sixty wins on PGA Tour, including four Masters, two British Opens, U.S. Open

A BALL'S A BALL

Professional athletes from other sports strut onto the golf course and discover they're duffers, just like everyone else.

My handicap? Woods and irons.

Chris Codiroli (1958–)
Professional baseball player

I was three over: one over a house, one over a patio and one over a swimming pool.

George Brett (1953–)
Hall of Fame baseball player

One of the advantages bowling has over golf is that you seldom lose a bowling ball.

Don Carter (1926–)
Hall of Fame bowler

It took me seventeen years
to get three thousand hits
in baseball. I did it in one
afternoon on the golf course.

Hank Aaron (1934–)
Professional baseball player

In baseball you hit your home run
over the right-field fence, the left-
field fence, the center-field fence.
Nobody cares. In golf everything has
got to be right over second base.

Ken Harrelson (1941–)
Professional baseball player

If I can hit a curveball,
why can't I hit a ball that is
standing still on a course?

Larry Nelson (1947–)
Winner of two PGA championships, U.S. Open

Golf is one of the few sports where it's possible to be really bad . . . and have a really good time.

Golf is so popular simply because it is the best game in the world at which to be bad.

A.A. Milne (1882–1956)
English author

It is more satisfying to be a bad player at golf. The worse you play, the better you remember the occasional good shot.

Nubar Gulbenkian (1896–1972)
British oil tycoon

One thing about golf is you don't know why you play bad and why you play good.

George Archer (1939–)
Won the 1969 Masters

Golf and sex are the only
things you can enjoy without
being good at them.

Jimmy Demaret (1910–)
First player to win the Masters three times

An interesting thing about
golf is that no matter how badly
you play, it is always
possible to get worse.

Author Unknown

Golf is a hard game to figure.
One day you'll go out and slice
it and shank it, hit into all the
traps and miss every green. The
next day you go out and for no
reason at all you really stink.

Author Unknown

There are no maladies
in my golf game. My
golf game stinks.

Jack Nicklaus (1940–)
All-time leader in major tournament
wins: twenty, including six Masters

Golf was once a rich
man's sport, but now it has
millions of poor players.

Author Unknown

I never knew what
top golf was like until
I turned professional.
Then it was too late.

Steve Melnyk (1947–)
Golf commentator

If you could eliminate the
occasional bad shot you would
be the first person to do so.

John Jacobs (1945–)
Professional golfer

It takes hundreds of good golf
shots to gain confidence, but
only one bad one to lose it.

Jack Nicklaus (1940–)
*All-time leader in major tournament
wins: twenty, including six Masters*

Doesn't it show us all that we are
silly little boys or fatuous asses to
think that we can play golf without
making a lot of bad shots?

Bobby Jones (1902–1971)
*Winner four U.S. Opens, five U.S. Amateurs,
three British Opens; founder of the Masters*

Why do we work so hard
to feel so terrible?

Hollis Stacy (1954–)
LPGA golfer

Golf is the only game where the worst
player gets the best of it. He obtains
more out of it as regards both exercise
and enjoyment, for the good player
gets worried over the slightest mistake,
whereas the poor player makes too
many mistakes to worry about them.

David Lloyd George (1863-1945)
British politician

No one has ever conquered this game.
One week out there and you are
God; next time you are the devil.

Juli Inkster (1960–)
LPGA golfer

NEVER GIVE UP!

No matter what happens—never give up a hole. In tossing in your cards after a bad beginning you also undermine your whole game, because to quit between tee and green is more habit-forming than drinking a highball before breakfast.

Sam Snead (1912–2003)
PGA Tour career victory leader: eighty-one wins

I've always made a total effort, even when the odds seemed entirely against me. I never quit trying; I never felt that I didn't have a chance to win.

Arnold Palmer (1929–)
Sixty wins on PGA Tour, including four Masters, two British Opens, U.S. Open

The biggest thing is to have the mind-set and the belief that you can win every tournament. Nicklaus had it.

Tiger Woods (1975–)
First golfer to hold all four major titles in a year

CHAMPIONS

ARNOLD PALMER

Arnold Palmer arrived on the professional golf scene along with television. He brought charisma and aggression to the game. His father, a groundskeeper and club pro, taught him to play golf at age three. With his powerful game style, he changed the perception that golf was not an athletic game. His physical strength and determination to always go for broke made Arnie a national hero. In 1968 he was the first man to win over one million dollars on the PGA tour. Few athletes have shared the special bond that Arnold Palmer enjoys with his fans. He is truly a man of the people, always stopping to give autographs, and "Arnie's Army" has appreciated and followed him for more than four decades. With his lifelong love affair with golf, he has helped to develop it into the industry it is today.

- *U.S. Amateur 1954*
- *U.S. Open 1960*
- *Masters 1958, 1960, 1962, 1964*
- *British Open 1961, 1962*
- *World Golf Hall of Fame 1974*

What other people may find in poetry or art museums, I find in the flight of a good drive.

Arnold Palmer (1929–)

COURSES

THE OLD COURSE

St. Andrew's . . . golf's oldest course and standing testament to the complexity and frustration of the game. Everybody hates it—and everybody wants to play there.

This is the origin of the game, golf in its purest form, and it's still played that way on a course seemingly untouched by time. Every time I play here, it reminds me that this is still a game.

Arnold Palmer (1929–)
Sixty wins on PGA Tour, including four Masters, two British Opens, U.S. Open

Until you play it, St. Andrews looks like the sort of real estate you couldn't give away.

Sam Snead (1912–2003)
PGA Tour career victory leader with eighty-one wins

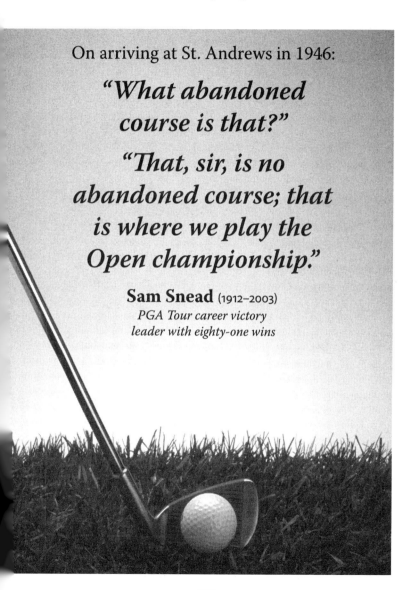

On arriving at St. Andrews in 1946:

"What abandoned course is that?"

"That, sir, is no abandoned course; that is where we play the Open championship."

Sam Snead (1912–2003)
PGA Tour career victory leader with eighty-one wins

Fifty Years of British Open Winners

2005	**Tiger Woods**		1980	**Tom Watson**
2004	**Todd Hamilton**		1979	**Seve Ballesteros**
2003	**Ben Curtis**		1978	**Jack Nicklaus**
2002	**Ernie Els**		1977	**Tom Watson**
2001	**David Duval**		1976	**Johnny Miller**
2000	**Tiger Woods**		1975	**Tom Watson**
1999	**Paul Lawrie**		1974	**Gary Player**
1998	**Mark O'Meara**		1973	**Tom Weiskopf**
1997	**Justin Leonard**		1972	**Lee Trevino**
1996	**Tom Lehman**		1971	**Lee Trevino**
1995	**John Daly**		1970	**Jack Nicklaus**
1994	**Nick Price**		1969	**Tony Jacklin**
1993	**Greg Norman**		1968	**Gary Player**
1992	**Nick Faldo**		1967	**Roberto de Vicenzo**
1991	**Ian Baker-Finch**		1966	**Jack Nicklaus**
1990	**Nick Faldo**		1965	**Peter Thomson**
1989	**Mark Calcavecchia**		1964	**Tony Lema**
1988	**Seve Ballesteros**		1963	**Bob Charles**
1987	**Nick Faldo**		1962	**Arnold Palmer**
1986	**Greg Norman**		1961	**Arnold Palmer**
1985	**Sandy Lyle**		1960	**Kel Nagle**
1984	**Seve Ballesteros**		1959	**Gary Player**
1983	**Tom Watson**		1958	**Peter Thomson**
1982	**Tom Watson**		1957	**Bobby Locke**
1981	**Bill Rogers**		1956	**Peter Thomson**

CHAMPIONS

HARRY VARDON

One of golf's first true superstars, Harry won six British Open championships, a feat still unmatched today. He was born on May 9, 1870 in Grouville, Jersey, and was a golf caddie by age seven, later following his brother's lead in going to England to become a professional. He never had a lesson, but had real natural talent. Harry developed the overlapping Vardon Grip which is used by ninety percent of players today.

- *U.S. Open 1900*
- *British Open 1896, 1898, 1899, 1903, 1911, 1914*
- *World Golf Hall of Fame 1974*

Golfers find it a very trying matter to
turn at the waist, more particularly
if they have a lot of waist to turn.

Harry Vardon (1870–1939)

THE U.S. OPEN

The only tournament a weekend warrior can enter, where nobodies become legend, and legends of the game are sometimes reduced to hacker status.

The fact that Slammin' Sammy couldn't win the Open made it all the more valuable for the players that did win. Gave it a special quality. I'd say a part of the sheen on that trophy comes from my sweat.

Sam Snead (1912–2003)
PGA Tour career victory leader with eighty-one wins

The U.S. Open flag eliminates a lot of players. Some players just weren't meant to win the U.S. Open. Quite often, they know it.

Jack Nicklaus (1940–)
All-time leader in major tournament wins with twenty, including six Masters

Fifty Years of U.S. Open Winners

2005 **Michael Campbell**	1980 **Jack Nicklaus**
2004 **Retief Goosen**	1979 **Hale Irwin**
2003 **Jim Furyk**	1978 **Andy North**
2002 **Tiger Woods**	1977 **Hubert Green**
2001 **Retief Goosen**	1976 **Jerry Pate**
2000 **Tiger Woods**	1975 **Lou Graham**
1999 **Payne Stewart**	1974 **Hale Irwin**
1998 **Lee Janzen**	1973 **Johnny Miller**
1997 **Ernie Els**	1972 **Jack Nicklaus**
1996 **Steve Jones**	1971 **Lee Trevino**
1995 **Corey Pavin**	1970 **Tony Jacklin**
1994 **Ernie Els**	1969 **Orville Moody**
1993 **Lee Janzen**	1968 **Lee Trevino**
1992 **Tom Kite**	1967 **Jack Nicklaus**
1991 **Payne Stewart**	1966 **Billy Casper**
1990 **Hale Irwin**	1965 **Gary Player**
1989 **Curtis Strange**	1964 **Ken Venturi**
1988 **Curtis Strange**	1963 **Julius Boros**
1987 **Scott Simpson**	1962 **Arnold Palmer**
1986 **Ray Floyd**	1961 **Gene Littler**
1985 **Andy North**	1960 **Arnold Palmer**
1984 **Fuzzy Zoeller**	1959 **Billy Casper**
1983 **Larry Nelson**	1958 **Tommy Bolt**
1982 **Tom Watson**	1957 **Dick Mayer**
1981 **David Graham**	1956 **Cary Middlecoff**

Playing in the U.S. Open is like tippy-toeing through hell.

Jerry McGee (1943–)

Professional golfer

THE AWESOME EIGHT

The World's Eight Superlative Courses

- **Hottest**   Alice Springs, Australia
  (summer temperatures 104°–108°)
- **Coldest**   North Star, Alaska
  (winter temperature -2°)
- **Most Northerly**   North Cape, Norway
- **Most Southerly**   Ushuaia, Argentina
- **Highest**   La Paz Golf Club, Bolivia
  (altitude 10,800 feet)
- **Lowest**   Furnace Creek, California
  (altitude -214 feet)
- **Toughest**   Ko'olau, Hawaii
  (par 72; 7,310 yards)
- **Greatest**   St. Andrews, Scotland

[Courses] should be difficult; secondly,
they should be pleasing to the eye;
thirdly, that they should be strictly
economical in design; and lastly,
that to be truly admirable they will
probably incur in the general opinion
the accusation of being unfair.

H.N. Wethered
Golf writer

HAZARDOUS DUTY

From the tee to the rough. From the rough to the creek. From the creek to the sand. We spend more time in the hazards than in the short grass. There's a lesson there, but it's hard to find.

I'm hitting the woods just great, but I'm having a terrible time getting out of them.

Harry Toscano (1943–)
Professional golfer

A rough should have high grass. When you go bowling they don't give you anything for landing in the gutter, do they?

Lee Trevino (1939–)
Two-time winner of three majors:
U.S. Open, British Open, PGA

If I had cleared the trees and drove the green, it would've been a great shot.

Sam Snead (1912–2003)
*PGA Tour career victory
leader with eighty-one wins*

Why is it twice as difficult to hit
a ball over water than sand?

Author Unknown

I'm in the woods so much I can
tell you which plants are edible.

Lee Trevino (1939–)
*Two-time winner of three majors:
U.S. Open, British Open, PGA*

You know what they say about big
hitters . . . the woods are full of them.

Jimmy Demaret (1910–)
First player to win the Masters three times

I'd like to see the fairways more narrow. Then everybody would have to play from the rough, not just me.

Seve Ballesteros (1957–)
Winner of three British Opens, two Masters

If you find yourself pleased that you locate more balls in the rough than you actually have lost, your focus is totally wrong and your personality might not be right for golf . . . it is also just a matter of time before the IRS investigates your business.

Author Unknown

A ball will always come to rest halfway down a hill, unless there is sand or water at the bottom.

Henry Beard
Humorist

cabbage: Thick rough

*The course of true golf
never did run smooth.*

Henny Youngman (1906–1998)
Comedian

CHAMPIONS

WALTER HAGEN

Walter Hagen, known as The Haig, was one of the most colorful characters the golfing world has ever seen. Born in New York on December 21, 1892, he entered golf as a caddie, and was as much a showman as an excellent golfer. He often said that he didn't want to be a millionaire, he only wanted to live like one, and he did. A full-time professional golfer, he shunned other jobs, even as a golf pro at a country club, to be on the course competing. Hagen was very self-confident, he accepted the bad shots the same as the good, and seldom lost his concentration.

- *U.S. Open 1914, 1919*
- *British Open 1922, 1924, 1928, 1929*
- *PGA 1921, 1924, 1925, 1926, 1927*
- *World Golf Hall of Fame 1974*

Give me a man with big hands
and big feet and no brains and I'll
make a golfer out of him.

Walter Hagen (1892–1969)

PHILOSOPHY OF COURSES

A golf course is the epitome of
all that is purely transitory in the
universe; a space not to dwell in, but
to get over as quickly as possible.

Jean Giraudoux (1882–1944)
French author, diplomat

Golf is not a fair game, so
why build a course fair?

Pete Dye
Course architect

Golf is probably the only known game
a man can play as long as a quarter
of a century and then discover it was
too deep for him in the first place.

Seymour Dunn
Early twentieth-century course designer

Being a Scotsman, I am naturally
opposed to water in its undiluted state.

Dr. Alistair Mackenzie (1870-1934)
Course designer

Golf courses are like children.
I have no favorite.

Robert Trent Jones (1906-2000)
Course designer

A good golf course makes you want
to play so badly that you hardly have
the time to change your shoes.

Ben Crenshaw (1952–)
Winner of two Masters

If you try to fight the course,
it will beat you.

Lou Graham (1938–)
Won the 1975 U.S. Open

THE NINETEENTH HOLE

All I've got against it is that it takes
you so far from the clubhouse.

Eric Linklater (1899–1974)
Scottish poet, author

I'll always remember the day I
broke ninety. I had a few beers in
the clubhouse and was so excited
I forgot to play the back nine.

Bruce Lansky
American author

The members who command the best
service at your golf club either have the
lowest handicaps or the highest bar bills.

Author Unknown

Where I play, the greens
always break toward the bar.

George Gobel (1919–1991)
Comedian

SAM SNEAD

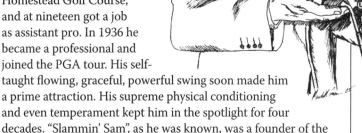

Famous for his folksy image and wearing a straw hat, Sam was a hill-billy mountain boy at heart. He was born on May 27, 1912, in Virginia. He got his start in golf by carving clubs from limbs of a swamp maple. He began caddying as a young boy at Homestead Golf Course, and at nineteen got a job as assistant pro. In 1936 he became a professional and joined the PGA tour. His self-taught flowing, graceful, powerful swing soon made him a prime attraction. His supreme physical conditioning and even temperament kept him in the spotlight for four decades. "Slammin' Sam", as he was known, was a founder of the U.S. Senior Tour.

- *PGA 1942, 1949, 1951*
- *Masters 1949, 1952, 1954*
- *British Open 1946*
- *World Golf Hall of Fame 1974*

> Forget your opponents;
> always play against par.

Sam Snead (1912–2003)

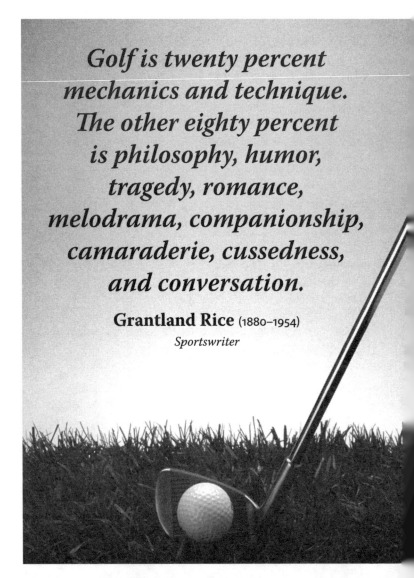

*Golf is twenty percent
mechanics and technique.
The other eighty percent
is philosophy, humor,
tragedy, romance,
melodrama, companionship,
camaraderie, cussedness,
and conversation.*

Grantland Rice (1880–1954)

Sportswriter

INDEX

ABOUT THE AUTHOR

When he's not chasing around a tiny ball with a stick, Christopher Armour (no relation to Tommy) is president of Armour&Armour Advertising and Publications in Nashville, Tennessee. Before founding the full-service agency, he worked at *The Tennessean* newspaper in Nashville in a variety of positions including sportswriter.

Armour is a 1978 graduate of Yale University. He's the author of several books, including *The Wisdom of Fishing* and *Forty Daily Devotions,* both published by Foxglove Press.

For more information, contact
Foxglove Press
939 Camp Nakanawa Road
Crossville, TN 38571
1-877-205-1932